GUIDE TO GOVERNMENT GRANTS & VENDOR OPPORTUNITIES

Harriet Grayson

Ocean Breeze Press

RI

Guide to Government Grants & Vendor Opportunities

Harriet Grayson

Published by Ocean Breeze Press

Rhode Island

Copyright 2014 by Harriet Grayson.

Manufactured in the United States of America

Library of Congress Cataloging-in-Publication Data Grayson, Harriet.

TABLE OF CONTENTS

CHAPTER 1

Introduction to Government Programs

Researching Federal Government opportunities

Organizations of all kinds including non-profits, universities/colleges, units of local & state government and small business can successfully apply for federal government grants as well as register as a government vendor. The largest grantor and buyer of goods and services in the country, possibly the world, is the US Federal Government. Government on all levels: federal, state and local offer both grants and vendor opportunities. On the federal level the government registration process to apply for grants and seek vendor contracting opportunities is similar and success in both spheres is possible. Government is a reliable business partner so don't neglect both grant and vendor contracting opportunities.

As you may expect government grant funding and vendor opportunities requires forms and procedures. This handy reference guide will provide information on:

- Researching government grant opportunities
- Registering with different government entities to be able to apply on-line
- Completing the various government forms required
- Constructing a grant application for submission
- Researching government vendor opportunities

Federal Government Grants

You may already know that the United States government has billions of dollars to distribute in the form of grants to entities of all kinds including all kinds of organizations including small business. You probably just don't know how to get your share of it. Government agencies also consist of quasi-government agencies such as transportation and housing authorities, historical commissions, water authorities, etc., which also offer grant and vendor opportunities.

Practically everybody is eligible to apply for government grants. This includes for-profit and non-profit organizations. The availability of federal grant funding and vendor opportunities are part of a larger political and economic cycle. The amounts fluctuate as do the priorities, but billions are still available from every federal government agency which then makes it available to the states and sometimes local units of government.

The big news was the arrival in 2009 of monies through "stimulus funds", otherwise known as the American Recovery & Reinvestment Act. The act was proposed by President Barack Obama and appropriated by the US Congress in early 2009 to the tune of almost $800 Billion. The money has been spent, the Congress changed players and bickering took the place of political negotiations so the federal government went without an actual budget for a couple of years. This led to uncertainty, and grant and vendor opportunities shrunk. In early 2014, the Congress passed and the President signed an actual 2-year budget. So moving forward more money should be available for grants and vendor opportunities for organizations of all kinds including small business.

These federal grant funds are available through an open competitive process, which increasingly relies upon a sophisticated online system currently used by more than 26 federal agencies. The system is designed to streamline an otherwise cumbersome process. In fact, most federal agencies are moving towards an exclusive on-line system although some agencies require both an on-line application and the mailing of supportive documentation such as audited financial statements and letters of support.

Traditionally, most government funding is linked to budget cycles usually reflecting the fiscal accounting cycle of the originating agency. For example, the federal fiscal year begins October 1st. Therefore many federal funding application deadlines, as well as the release of funding are tied to that fiscal cycle. A grant application referring to federal FY2015 means that the funding cycle begins October 1, 2014 and ends September 30, 2015. State governments operate on a different fiscal cycle; likewise grants are more likely to be announced and rewarded based on the state cycles. All but four states run their fiscal years from July 1 to June 30. The four exceptions are: New York and Texas which run their fiscal cycles from April 1 through March 31st, and Alabama and Michigan operate their fiscal cycles identical to the federal fiscal cycle, October 1 through September 30th.

Sometimes what happens is that there are more favorable applications than there is money available. So applications can receive passing grades from government reviewers but not be funded due to a lack of money. The result is that the organizations may indeed be sent an award letter and then later another letter indicating that the application would have been funded had additional funds been available.

Suggestion -- never hire or enter into a contract or purchase expensive equipment based on a favorable review or receipt of an award letter unless your organization actually receives a signed contract from the originating government agency.

Free Money – Don't be Deceived. No free lunch

There are endless promotions seen on TV and the internet, heard on the radio and sometimes to be found in the classified sections of newspapers proclaiming "free government grants available". This is all hype and verges on fraud. Yes, government grants are available but they are not that easy to get and they all come with strings attached. To protect the taxpayer's money, your money, the government doesn't willy-nilly give away funds. The money is not for the taking. However, if your organizations has a good idea that fits within the guidelines provided by the grantor agency, practices sound accounting methods, employs experienced staff and can submit on time and within page limitations a reasonable grant application, government grant funding is possible. It's not simple but it's possible and the more an organization submits applications, the more likely they will eventually get funding. More submitted applications is better than less. Practice makes perfect. And success breeds success. Once the organization has received that first grant contract, has established a record of sound accounting and documented performance standards, the next government grant becomes that much easier to obtain.

Opportunities: RFP – PA – RFA

A RFP (Request for Proposal), Public Announcement (PA) or RFA (Request for Application) are the most commonly found grant opportunity announcements. However, government agencies do use other terms. The federal Department of Housing and Urban Development uses the term Notices of Funding Availabilities (NOFA). Other examples: the federal Department of Justice requests "Solicitations" while the federal Environmental Protection Agency may announce RFIP (Request for Initial Grant Proposals) because many of their initial announcements are used as screening devices. The organization submits a first application and a majority of those applications are rejected. Those remaining applicants then submit a more detailed application for the actual funding. State agencies may simply refer to a grant opportunity as a PA (Program Announcement).

Researching Federal Government Grant Opportunities

There are good online sites to look at for grant opportunities, but there is no one site that lists them all. The federal government has become more technologically sophisticated in recent years so that a variety of RFPs, PAs or RFAs can be located on the major federal grant site – www.grants.gov. The federal government's Federal Service Desk for the above web site operates 24 hours a day, 7 days a week except on Federal holidays. The number is 800-518-4726. Never hesitate to ask for help. Your tax money pays for the service.

The web site has recently been upgraded and enhanced making it easier to research opportunities. You can quickly ascertain how many grants are available and obtain specific information on each grant.

Starting with the website www.grants.gov check the page "Search Grants." There you can find search tools: Keyword(s), Funding Opp # and CFDA Number. The keywords would be words such as arts, community development, small business, and many others. All grants are organized by the federal government into the classification system called Catalog of Federal Domestic Assistance (CFDA) which covers 2,270 different federal programs. Funding Opp # refers to the federal government's assignment of a specific number for each grant. Usually the actual number contains letters indicating the federal agency and the date of the grant (14 appears somewhere within the Funding Opp # indicating 2014 the current year).

Also very helpful to anyone searching for grants on this *"Search Grants"* page is the left-hand column which has information on:

- Opportunity Status

- Eligibility

- Category

- Agency

The "Opportunity Status" includes the number of open grants, which changes regularly as more new grants are announced and grant deadlines are reached. It is a handy reference tool because it quickly measures the robustness of grant opportunities.

"Eligibility" is the most important first step in determining grant opportunities because the federal government explicitly indicates which types of groups are eligible to apply for a grant. Most grants permit more than one type of group to apply. Exceptions to this rule are those grants specifically targeted to state government and those that are continuation grants. There are numerous eligibility categories listed below:

- City or township governments

- County government

- For profit organizations other than small businesses

- Independent school districts

- Individuals

- Native American tribal governments & organizations

- Private public & state controlled institutions of higher education

- Public housing authorities

- Small businesses

- Special district governments

- State government

Then there is something called "Category" which is similar in concept to keywords. The list is numerous but helps the seeker to quickly find appropriate grant opportunities.

- Agriculture

- Arts

- Business & commerce

- Consumer Protection

- Disaster Prevention & Relief

- Education

- Employment, Labor & training

- Energy

- Environment

- Food & Nutrition

- Health (largest number of grant opportunities)

- Housing

- Humanities

- Income Security & Social Services

- Information & Statistics

- Law, Justice & Legal Services

- Natural Resources

- Regional Development

- Science & Technology

- Transportation

Also to facilitate grant searching there is a classification by actual federal "Agency." So if the potential grantee is interested in grant opportunities from a specific federal agency the process is made easier. The agencies listed are as follows:

- Agency for International Development

- Department of Agriculture

- Department of Commerce

- Department of Defense

- Department of Energy

- Department of Health & Human Services

- Department of Homeland Security

- Department of Housing & Urban Development

- Department of Justice

- Department of Labor

- Department of State

- Department of Interior

- Department of Treasury

- Department of Veterans Affairs

- Environmental Protection Agency

- National Aeronautics & Space Administration

- National Achieves & Records

- National Endowment for the Humanities

- National Endowment for the Arts

- National Science Foundation (largest number of grants)

- Small Business Administration

The largest funding source in the United States is the federal government. The majority of grant opportunities are awarded to organizations that have previously received federal funding. However, the federal government is always seeking to expand its list of grantees, if for no other reason than it looks better politically. It is unlikely for a brand new organization (under one year) to receive federal grant funding because an important element in a successful award is demonstrated fiscal responsibility. The federal government determines this by reviewing the organization's financial statements.

. However, one should never assume that this site has all grant opportunities listed, so it is always advisable to also directly search the web site of specific federal agencies such as Health and Human Services (HHS) or Housing and Urban Development (HUD), which operates 35 programs and authorized $1 Billion in grants last year. These are very large federal agencies with multiple levels of agencies under these behemoths. It is equally important to search out grants directly announced by sub-agencies.

For example, HHS is the largest federal agency and is the parent of 11 big and important grantor agencies:

- Administration for Children and Families (ACF)Administration on Aging (AoA),

- Food and Drug Administration (FDA)

- National Institutes of Health (NIH)

- Centers for Disease Control & Prevention (CDC)

- Agency for Healthcare Research & Quality (AHRQ)

- Agency for Toxic Substance & Disease Registry (ATSDR)

- Health Resources & Services Administration (HRSA)

- Indian Health Services (HIS)

- Centers for Medicare & Medicaid Services

- Substance Abuse & Mental Health Services Administration (SAMHSA)

Geography

Certain RFPs are released for specific geographical regions. The federal government has ten regions and RPF's are announced that cover only specified regions, sometimes only a specific state is mentioned so only potential awardees located in these geographic areas should apply. Carefully read any announcements to ascertain if there are geographic limitations.

10 Federal Regions

Region 1: CT, ME, MA, NH, RI, VT

Region 2: NJ, NY

Region 3: DE, DC, MD, PA, VA, WV

Region 4: AL, FL, GA, KY, MS, NC, SC, TN

Region 5: IL, IN, MI, MN, OH, WI

Region 6: AR, LA, NM, OK, TX

Region 7: IA, KS, MO, NE

Region 8: CO, MT, ND, SD, UT, WY

Regions 9: AZ, CA, HI, NV

Region 10: AK, ID, OR, WA

Location matters in other ways. Certain federal grants such as those awarded by the Office of Justice, (US Department of Justice) pre-determine locations where the funding can be awarded based on crime statistics or where "pilot" or "seed" programs have already received initial funding. In a similar way, certain health grants are awarded to locations where there is a high incidence of certain health problems. So before embarking on an elaborate plan for completing an application, check these other factors. Does your organization's project reflect meeting the required statistics?

In RFPs that have a research element there may be other eligibility requirements. For example, federal research grants require that the applicant's principal investigator(s) – PI demonstrate the necessary research and academic credentials. To successful compete for this funding, the application must clearly show this fact, usually with a carefully constructed resume or curriculum vitae (c.v.). If the application requires a specific type of training; for example, completion of a course by the Centers for Disease Control & Prevention (CDC) then the resume must reflect this training. Most federal grants that require the expertise of a PI will also require that the PI be registered. This is an additional process to the on-line registration process that will be discussed later.

Contact Your Federal Representatives

The next important step in successfully obtaining government grant funding is to better understand the federal granting bureaucracy by seeking out your organization's federal representation in the US House of Representatives and the US Senate. It's easy and extremely valuable to know who these men and woman are for the organization's financial well-being. For the US House of Representatives go to www.writerep.house.gov and locate your representative. The drop-down menus are simple to follow. First, indicate the state or territory, enter your zip code and, this is a must, the 4-digit code extension. If you don't know this 4-digit code extension number go to the United States Postal Service's web site for the information: www.usps.gov.

Find the local staff person that is a contact point. Most Congressional representatives have very fine and responsive local staff that is there to assist with constituents' problems and questions. If your organization is unknown to the district office staff, invite them to your offices and let them see or learn about what contribution your Oorganization is making to the community. Ask the Congressional staff in the district office if they have suggestions of contact people in federal agencies and specific web sites to utilize regarding grant opportunities. The US House of Representatives is known as the "People's House" because they are more likely to be approachable than the US Senate.

However, don't neglect to contact your US Senators. The web site is www.us.senate.gov. Use the drop-down menus to locate your organization's two Senators. Each Senator has his/her own web page and search it for the local staff person. Also, if the Senator is a Chair of an important Senate Committee or sub-Committee that impacts your organization's mission or services locate a staff contact to discuss future grant opportunities. Most Senators and Congress people have created e-mail newsletters. In some cases, these newsletters announce grant opportunities. Be sure to sign up for all available newsletters.

Getting Started with the Federal On-line Registration Process

Applying On-Line as an Organization (non-profit, government entity, business)

The government application process has joined the twenty-first century, permitting a number of federal agencies to accept grant applications electronically. However, there is a registration process that must be followed. Again, these are not difficult steps, but it does demand thinking ahead of the deadline. There are five steps to follow. The process for each step varies and can take from one day to two weeks so plan well in advance to submit an electronic federal grant application. Start with the grants.gov website and the page "Applicants" and then follow to "Applicant Resources" and from there "Organization Registration."

The government web site indicates that the process can take as little as 3-5 business days but usually expect longer delays especially if this is a first time registration. The grants.gov web site states, "NOTE: Registration takes, approximately 3-5 business days; but, allow 4 weeks to complete all steps."

Step 1: Obtain DUNS Number

Obtaining a DUNS number is relatively easy. The federal government has adopted the use of DUNS numbers as their way of tracking the federal grant allocations. It takes no more than one day to accomplish this step. Can be done on-line or via the phone. The number if you choose to apply via telephone is 866-705-5711. The process is *FREE* so under no circumstances should your organization be charged a fee. Your organization will also be required to have a Taxpayer Identification Number (TIN); this is usually the Employer Identification Number (EIN) provided by the IRS and used when filing a tax return.

DUNS (Data Universal Number System) **Number registration requires the following:**

- Name of the organization

- Phone number

- Name of the CEO/Executive Director of Organization

- Legal structure (corporation, partnership, proprietorship, non-profit)

- Year the Organization started

- Primary line of business/Organization's services

- Total number of employees (full and part-time)

Step 2: Register with SAM (System for Award Management)

The on-line system requires an applicant to register with SAM (change as of July 2012; in the past organizations registered with CCR). If this is a first time applying for federal grants highly recommended to participate in the SAM Webinar.

The process starts by going to web site: www.sam.gov. In the SAM, system organizations regardless of whether they are a business, non-profit they are referred to as "entity." Click on "Register with SAM" and then "Create a SAM Individual User Account"(be sure to validate your email address), then Log in. Select "Register New entity" under "Register/Update Entity" on the "My SAM" page. Select your type of entity. The definitions are in the glossary on the right. If you are registering in SAM.gov so you can only apply for a Federal grant and <u>NOT</u> interested in pursuing Federal contracts the process is much shorter.

To choose the "grants only" path: Select "No" to "Do you wish to bid on contracts?" Select "Yes' to "Do you want to be eligible for grants and other federal assistance?"

Complete the "Core Data" pages:

- Validate your DUNS information.

- Enter Business Information (TIN, etc.). This page is also where you create your Marketing Partner Identification

Number (MPIN). Write the MPIN down and keep it in a safe and accessible place. It will serve as a password for you in other government systems, you will need it for your grants.gov registration.

- Enter your Cage code if you have one. Cage Codes are tied to DUNS numbers and cannot be reused. Don't worry if you don't have a Cage Code for the DUNS number you are registering, one will be assigned to you after your registration is submitted.

- Enter General Information (business types, organization structure, etc.) about your entity.

- Provide your entity's Financial Information i.e. US bank Electronic Funds Transfer (EFT) information for Federal government payment purposes.

- Answer the executive Compensation questions.

- Answer the Proceedings Details questions.

- Next step is to complete the "Points of Contact" pages:

Your Electronic Business POC (E-Biz) is integral to your grants.gov registration and application process. Your Government POC will be used by other government systems such as CAGE, when they contact you. List someone with direct knowledge of this registration for both of those POCs.

Then make sure to hit (Submit) after your final review. You will get a "Congratulations" message on the screen. If you do not see this message you have not submitted your registration

There are two external validation steps one with IRS and another with CAGE, after you submit. You will receive

IMPORTANT: Your Organization needs to renew this SAM registration annually. You cannot continue to Step 3 without an up-to-date SAM registration.

Step 3: Username & Password

The person authorized to submit grant applications, the AOR ("Authorized Organization Representative").needs to complete an on-line profile and create a username and password, which will serve as their "electronic signature." Without completing this process an organization cannot submit electronic applications. If the organization is small, the E-Biz POC and the AOR can be the same person although it requires an alternate email than the one used to register as an E-Biz POC. After your Organization registers with SAM, AORs must wait one business day before completing their profile. Once the profile is submitted that same day the AOR should be able to use their username and password.

Step 4: AOR Authorization

Once the AOR has registered, the E-Biz POC will receive an e-mail notification from Grants.gov. and an e-mail copy is sent to the AOR. Then the E-Biz POC must login to Grants.gov (using the Organization's DUNS number for the username and the MPIN password – process described in Step 2) and approve the AOR. This is the official step that permits the AOR to submit applications for the

Organization. Only the E-Biz POC can approve AORs. It is always prudent in designating AORs to select someone reliable. Immediately after the E-Biz POC logs-in and approves the AOR, the person can begin submitting grant applications.

Step 5: Track AOR Status

The AOR can track the status of their authorization by logging in to Grants.gov using their username and password (obtained through the process in Step 3) and learn whether the E-Biz POC has approved their authorization.

This may seem like a cumbersome process but it is really very useful if your Organization intends to apply for multiple grants with agencies that are listed. Eventually, all federal agencies will be on this system. Remember there is a Help Desk 800-518-4726 and go back to the tutorial if you are confused or uncertain.

Federal Government Application Forms

While the federal application process appears daunting, it is largely the completion of a series of forms followed by the creation of a project narrative and the development of a budget with a budget justification. Almost all federal applications start with Standard Form 424 - SF 424 (frequently revised but always the latest is available through the on-line application system), which is known as the Application for Federal Assistance.

In order to complete this form, your Organization has to have accomplished several other steps along the way. Every application requires Employer Identification Number (EIN) and a DUNS identification number which is required for the registration process discussed above.

The Form 424 also requires listing the Congressional District of the applicant as well as where the project is located. Usually a grant announcement has a title and an accompanying Catalog of Federal Domestic Assistance Number (CFDA). You must include this number on the Form 424. Also, the Form 424 requests a geographic description of where the project will be located – city, county, state, etc. As part of the documentation for any government grant application, it's always advisable to include demographics and if possible, a map delineating the physical geography of the project.

Other Forms

The federal government wants assurances that your Organization follows the restrictions, regulations and laws that have been enacted. Standard Form 424B is the "Assurances – Non-Construction Programs." This form is an all-in-one legal promise that your Organization can fulfill all the requirements of the particular grant you are seeking. It demands that the Organization comply with all Federal statues regarding nondiscrimination. The language of Form 424B speaks to federal laws such as Title VI of the Civil Rights Act of 1964, Title IX of the Education Amendments of 1972, Section 504 of the Rehabilitation Act of 1973, Age Discrimination Act of 1975, Drug Abuse Office and Treatment Act of 1972, Comprehensive Alcohol Abuse and Alcoholism Prevention, Treatment and Rehabilitation Act of 1970. This language is standard legalese and should not present any problems; however, if your Organization has been cited for discrimination or there is a pending lawsuit, then you should consult your attorney and review carefully the language of these assurances.

Other issues addressed in Form 424B include compliance with the federal Hatch Act limiting political activities of employees: Davis-Bacon Act sets labor standards, environmental standards under a series of federal laws and the catch-all phrase: "Will comply with all applicable requirements of all other Federal laws, executive orders, regulations and policies governing this program." Unless your Organization has been cited for violations under federal law, the only important assurance that you must be prepared to accept is the Organization's willingness to meet required financial and compliance audits in accordance with the Single Audit Act of 1984. In other words, be prepared, and expect to be audited by the federal government.

The "Certifications" Sheet is similar to Form 424B. It contains language concerning five certifications or what can be referred to as declarations. "Certification 1" refers to debarment and suspension. This certification asks if the Organization been debarred, suspended, declared ineligible for federal funding because of fraud or some other criminal act. "Certification 2" deals with maintaining a drug-free workplace. "Certification 3" concerns the prohibition against lobbying. "Certification 4" certifies that all the statements given are true, complete and accurate. "Certification 5" refers to maintaining a smoke free environment.

The issue of lobbying is important for the federal government. In addition to the Certifications Form there is a specific form called the "Disclosure of Lobbying Activities," which must be completed.

A private organization must be prepared to demonstrate evidence of their organizations status. The easiest proof is to provide a copy of a valid Internal Revenue Service 501(c)(3) Letter of Determination.

Letter of Intent (LOI)

In the RFP announcement, there can be a statement about submitting a Letter of Intent (LOI) prior to filing an application. Submitting an LOI is not a binding obligation by an applicant to submit an application. But there are certain advantages for doing so. For some government agencies, the LOI is meant as a means of determining the level of interest of prospective applicants. In most cases, the LOI is nothing more than a statement that the organization is interested in the RFP. If there is more than one type of proposal announced, then the applicant is asked to check a box indicating interest in Component A versus Component B or interest in both parts of the RFP. Usually, the grantor agency actually provides a sample LOI and it can be faxed or sent by e-mail. It's that easy.

However, in some cases the grantor agency may use the LOI as a way of culling through many potential applicants. It will be much more than a sample letter but several pages in length outlining the proposed project or program. In those cases, the LOI is mandatory and requires the applicant to have a solid idea about the prospective application. Review the requirements concerning the LOI carefully. It may state categorically that without submitting an LOI, an organization is prohibited from later filing an application.

It is always advisable, even if there is no requirement to file a LOI, to go ahead and submit one. It is not a binding document, so if the organization chooses later not to submit the LOI, it's fine. It usually doesn't take too much time and it immediately puts your organization on the agency's mailing list so that any changes to the RFP or modifications will be sent to your Organization.

Deadlines are Crucial

The above statement cannot be emphasized enough – deadlines are crucial. Observe not only the day a grant application is due but also the time of the day. Deadline times can be listed as end of the business day – you need to find out what time that is. More commonly a specific time will be on the RFP. Typically these times are either 4 or 5 PM, but they can be noon. Most federal agencies are located in the Eastern Time zone so if your organization is on the west coast make certain that application is received on time.

Letters of Intent have deadlines which also must be respected. Forwarding backup documentation is sometimes required on a RFP. These requirements can have different deadlines but usually the timetable is within two weeks, no longer than 30 days after submitting the actual application. The easiest way to discard prospective applicants by the grantor agency is the failure of the organization to submit the application on time. One of the great virtues of on-line applications is that there are no postal or private delivery service complications. However, computers can fail so that's why even in a world of on-line applications it is most desirable to submit the application at least two days in advance of that deadline.

Federal Government Software Requirements

There are software applications that allow you to successfully navigate the Grants.gov pages and complete your application. Check the Grants.gov web site "Support" and then click "Technical Support" and then "Recommended Software" to ensure that your application can be properly submitted.

CHAPTER 2

Introduction to Federal Government Vendor Opportunities

Researching federal government vendor opportunities

Organizations of all kinds including small business, non-profits, public and private universities and colleges, units of government, individuals can successfully apply to become federal government vendors. The process requires registering as a vendor similar to becoming registered to apply for federal grants. Also similar to grants.gov the process is centralized through a web-based site; the web site is: www.fedbizopps.gov.

Federal Government Vendor Opportunities

The web site fedbizopps.gov is the place to start for searching for vendor opportunities and applying to become a federal government vendor. At any given time the number of vendor opportunities fluctuates but is usually more than 25,000 separate entries. All federal government contracts between $3,000 - $150,000 are automatically reserved for small business.

The home page of the web site fedbizopps.gov provides an enormous amount of information. First, there are the search engine components. These include the following:

- Posted date
- Set-Aside Code
- Place of Performance
- Type of Solicitation
- Key word/Solicitation #

- Agency

Searching for Federal Vendor Opportunities - Elements

Posted Date

You can review vendor opportunities by specific time periods: Today (the actual day you are visiting the site), last 2 Days, 3 Days, 7 Days, 14 Days, 21 Days, 30 Days, 90 Days, 180 Days, 365 Days (one year). It is possible to see trends in the vendor opportunities. For example, if you look at "Today" how many opportunities are there versus 180 days ago and type of vendor opportunities?

Set-Aside Programs

The federal government has created a number of what it calls "Set-Aside" programs that provide opportunities for certain very specific groups of small business owners, primarily, economically and socially disadvantaged or veterans or women small business owners.. If your small business fits into one of these "Set-Aside" categories that means the federal government has carved out of its trillion dollar contractor programs money just for these groups. One of the chief advantages of being certified into one of these special categories is that instead of openly competitive contracts there is the availability of sole source contracts – no open bidding. Different industries have different standards of what constitutes a small business. In most cases the maximum small business size is one with less than 500 employees. The following are the type of groups and key element of the programs:

- Competitive 8(a)
- Emerging Small Business
- HubZone
- Women Owned Small Business
- Service-Disabled Vet-Owned Small Business
- Total HBCU/MI

Competitive 8(a)

What is the Competitive 8(a) program? It is designed for small business owners who are economically or socially disadvantaged (refers to Section 8(a) of the Small Business Act). This can include the typical racial groupings but beyond that geographic isolation and those physically handicapped. The program provides access to capital and credit, business counseling and training, and contracting opportunities. There are 10,000 firms with more than $10 billion in federal government contracts certified under this program.

To qualify for the program the business must be in existence at least two years. A business can remain in the program for as many as nine (9) years. Under this program a small business can receive sole source contracts for up to $4 million in goods/services and $6.5 million for manufacturing. Also encouraged is for the small business to seek out and form joint ventures and teaming with other small businesses. At least 51% of the firm must be owned and controlled by US citizens.

In addition, to qualify individual business owners must have a net worth of less than $250,000 excluding the business and one's personal residence. Once the business is certified the individual owners' net worth value can increase to $750,000.

Emerging Small Business

The Emerging Small Business Program is designed for businesses no larger than 50% of the applicable small business standard. The set-aside contract value is for $30,000 or less.

HUBZone

HUBZone refers to Historically Underutilized Business Zone and is designed for small businesses in economically distressed communities to obtain federal contracts. This is a geographic area with high unemployment (at least 140% of the state's average) or low-income (80% of the non-metropolitan state median household income). To qualify a business must be small (less than 500 employees), be 51% owned and controlled by US citizens, have its principle office in a HUBZone and have at least 35% of the employees residing in a HUBZone.

There are HUBZones across the country in both urban and rural areas. The SBA lists the designated HUBZones (9,000 urban census tracts, 900 rural counties and all Native American reservations). It is best to check with the SBA to determine whether the business site is within a HUBZone. .

Women Owned Small Business (WOSB)

Qualifications for businesses in this set-aside program are those owned 51% by one or more women who all must be US citizens. The business can self-certify for this program or use the services of designated Third Party Certifiers. These include the following: El Paso Hispanic Chamber of Commerce, National Women Business Owners Corp, US Women's Chamber of Commerce and Women's Business Enterprise National Council.

WOSB became effective on April 1, 2011. It provides for manufacturing and other types of services. Until 2013 there were financial limits to those contracts but those have been eliminated. Unlike other types of set-aside programs this category does not permit sole source contracts.

The set-aside program for WOSBs is designed to assist women owned small businesses to succeed in industries where traditionally they have not been represented. So to this end the contracts are directed at 83 industries; 45 where women owned small businesses are underrepresented and 38 where women owned small businesses are substantially underrepresented. Most of these industries involve manufacturing. For example, in the underrepresented category the manufacturing is in areas such as residential building, apparel, architectural & structural metals, communications equipment, etc. Other industries include: facilities support services, investigative and security services automotive repair and maintenance, etc. In the substantially underrepresented category the manufacturing industries are chemical, coating & engraving, household and institutional furniture, office furniture, etc. Other substantially underrepresented industries include freight trucking, warehousing and storage, newspaper publishing, software publishing, scientific research, etc. The SBA maintains a specific list of the industries.

In order to participate in the program the women owned small business must:

- Register with System for Award Management (SAM) same as with grants.gov
- Register with SBA's General Login System (GLS)
  - Create User ID
  - Complete Identity Info
  - Complete Contact ID
- Complete all documents on WOSB program repository

Service Disabled Veteran Owned Small Business Concern Program (SDVOSBC)

The SDVOSBC was enacted into law on December 16, 2003 by President Bush under the Veterans Benefits Act of 2003. It is similar in design and qualifications as a business in the HUBZone program.

To be eligible for the program the small business must be 51% owned by someone with a service-connected disability that has been determined by the Department of Veterans Affairs or the Department of Defense. The management and day-to-day operation and control of the small business must be by a service-disabled veteran.

HBCU/MI

This program is for Historically Black Colleges and Universities and Minority Institutions

Place of Performance

This refers to the place where the contracting will take place and includes the 50 states, District of Columbia (DC) and US territories.

Type of Solicitation

There are many types of solicitations. But if your aim is to search for an overall view of what is being sought by the federal government select "Any" and see the largest pool of potential opportunities. There is also a Type of Solicitation that provides information on "Sale of Surplus Property" so if your organization is searching for any number of different kinds of items (e.g., cars, office furniture, boats, computers, and buildings) peruse this site.

There are also search indicators by "Agency" if you are seeking specific federal agency contracting and also "Keyword/Solicitation #" is you know exactly the contracting opportunity of interest to your organization.

Searching for Federal Vendor Opportunities - Alternative Approach

There is more than one way to search for federal government vendor opportunities. An alternative approach is to go to the federal government vendor web site: www.fedbizopps.gov and check the right lower corner of the opening page. There you will see "Vendors/Citizens" section of the web site. On the left side of the section is a request to input your Username & Password. You will eventually need to establish a username & password to register as a federal government vendor but *NOT* to simply review the potential vendor opportunities. On the right area of this section there is the "Find Opportunities" – just click on that line.

Once you click "Find Opportunities" the site directs you to the federal government vendor opportunities posted within the last 90 days. There will be thousands. The ninety days can be changed; it is a drop down menu and the default is 90 days but it can be replaced with one day or as long as 365 days. You can make that choice.

The default is also for "All in Descending Order" of the posting date. Again you can change that via the drop down menu. You may wish to check by the name of a specific federal agency or by "Set Aside." This would give you a review of all "Set-Aside" programs (see above for discussion of federal government "Set-Aside" programs).

The default is to review twenty (20) different vendor opportunities per page. Again this is a drop down menu and can be changed. . When the opportunities are listed on the screen,click on a specific opportunity. What comes up is a page providing important basic information. This new page contains information on:

- Solicitation Number
- Notice Type
- Synopsis
- Request for Proposal letter (download)
- All the attachments associated with this particular vendor opportunity (downloads)
- Primary & Secondary contact Info (name, email address & telephone #)

Listed is the essential information that indicates whether the organization wants to actually submit a bid to the federal government.

Registering as a Vendor – Getting Started

Registering is easy. The federal vendor registration system asks for a DUNS# similar to www.grants.gov. You can obtain a DUNS# without cost and relatively quickly. See Chapter 1 for details (free phone number and procedures). However, if you want to just register, you can do so without a DUNS# but it will limit what types of materials you can receive from the federal government to submit a bid. I strongly suggest every organization obtain a DUNS#.

The next step is to complete Company Information:

- Legal Business Name*
- Doing Business as (DBA)*
- Cage #
- Division Name
- Division Number
- Physical Address (Street, Street #, City State, Zip + 4, Country*
- Mailing Address (same as above)*

This is followed by Personal Information

- Group Name
- Full Name*
- Suffix
- Title
- Email Address*
- Phone Number*
- Username*
- Password (specific length, lower case & upper case letters, numbers, symbols)*

*required

The final step is a quick and simple Email Verification, which you must respond to in order to activate your account. Now you are ready to learn about federal government vendor opportunities, read about the specifications in order to submit a bid, and if the opportunity seems promising then submit a bid.

CHAPTER 3

State Grant & Vendor Opportunities

Researching state government grant opportunities

Organizations of all kinds including non-profits, universities/colleges, units of local government and small business can successfully apply for state government grants as well as register as a state government vendor. However unlike the federal government, seeking state grant opportunities requires some serious searching because there is no constantly updated on-line web-based system. It is far more haphazard and requires searching throughout the state webs sites including at specific state agencies for information. It may be far more effective to work with state elected officials to learn when new grant opportunities become available.

Researching state government vendor opportunities

Unlike grant opportunities, learning how to do business with state government is often an easy and highly accessible process on every state's web site. Most state government official web sites list specific details on how to register as a state government vendor and searching out potential opportunities.

Specific state web site information

Listing by state of official state web sites, state agency information links and vendor opportunity links. All listings are subject to change since most state governments on-line webs sites continue to evolve.

Alabama

www.alabama.gov (Alabama Agency and Organization Listing)

Division of Procurement, Department of Finance

http://purchasing.alabama.gov

Vendor Registration

http://purchasing.alabama.gov/pages/vendors.aspx

Disadvantaged Business Enterprise (DBE) Program

www.dot.state.al.us/bureau/hr/dbe/default.asp

Alaska

www.alaska.gov (My Government)

Department of Administration, General Services

www.doa.alaska.gov/dgs/

DBE Program

www.dot.state.ak.us/cvlrts/directory.shtml

Arizona

Az.gov (State agencies Directory - az.gov/app/contactaz)

Department of Administration

www.azdoa.gov/agencies/spo/business_resoruces.asp

Harriet Grayson

ProcureAZ eProcurement System

https://procure.az.gov/bso/

DBE Program

www.azdot.gov/azdbe/index.asp

Arkansas

www.arkansas.gov (State Directory)

Department of Finance and Administration

www.dfa.arkansas.gov/Pages/default.aspx

Vendor Services

www.ark.org/vendor/index.html

DBE Program

www.arkansas.gov/adfa/programs/dbep.html

California

www.ca.gov (ca.gov/casearch/agencies.aspx)

Procurement Division

www.pd.dgs.ca.gov/default.htm

Contracts Register

www.eprocure.dgs.ca.gov/default.htm

Organizations & DVBE services – Organizations/disabled vets (state program) www.pd.dgs.ca.gov/smbus/default.htm

DBE Program

www.dot.ca.gov/hq/bep/

Colorado

www.colorado.gov (State Agencies)

Department of Personnel & Administration

www.colorado.gov/dpa/dfp/spo/index.htm?opendocument

Vendor Registration

www.gssa.state.co.us/VenRegister

DBE Program

www.dot.state.co.us/EEO/DBEProgramPage.htm

Connecticut

www.ct.gov   (State   Agencies   -
ct.gov/ctportal/cwp/view.asp?)

Department of Administrative Services

www.das.state.ct.us/Purchase/New_PurchHome/Busopp.as
p

Contracting Portal to search for Bid/RFP solicitations,
contract

www.das.state.ct.us/Purchase/portal/portal_home.asp

Minority & Organizations Set-Aside Program (state
program)

www.state.ct.us/das/Purchase/SetAside/SAProgin.htm

Delaware

www.delaware.gov (List of Agencies - delaware.gov/topics/agencylist)

Government Support Services

http://gss.omb.delaware.gov/contracting/index.shtml

Office of Minority & Women Business Enterprise (state program)

http://omwbe.delaware.gov/certify.shtml

DBE Program

http://deldot.gov/information/business/dbe/index.shtml

Florida

www.myflorida.com (Find an Agency)

Florida Purchasing Division

http://dms.myflorida.com/business_operations/state_purchasing

Florida Office of Supplier Diversity (state program)

http://dms.myflorida.com/other_programs/office_of_suppl ier_diveristy_osd/

DBE Program

www.dot.state.fl.us/equalopportunityoffice/

Georgia

Georgia.gov (Agencies)

Department of Administrative Services

http://doas.ga.gov/StateLocal/SPD/Pages/Home.aspx

Vendor Registration

http://doas.georgia.gov/Suppliers/Pages/Home.aspx

Minority Business Enterprise Certification (state program)

http://doas.georgia.gov/Suppliers/Pages/SupplierMBE.asp
x

DBE Program

www.dot.state.ga.us/doingbusiness/dbePrograms/Pages/default.
aspx

Hawaii

www.hawaii.gov (Agencies)

State Procurement Office

www.spo.hawaii.gov/

Hawaii State & County Procurement Notices

http://www4.hawaii.gov/bidapps/

DBE Program

http://hawaii.gov/dot/administration/ocr/dbe

Idaho

www.idaho.gov (Agency & Topic Index - idaho.gov/agency/agency_a.html)

Department of Administration

http://adm.idaho.gov/purchasing/

Vendor Registration

http://www.sicomm.net/

DBE Program

www.itd.idaho.gov/civil/overview.htm

Harriet Grayson

Illinois

www.illinois.gov **(State Agencies - www2.illinois.gov/pages/agencies)**

Sell 2 Illinois – Business Registration

http://sell2.illinois.gov/

Organizations Set-Aside Program (state program)

http://sell2.illinois.gov/SBSP/Small_Businesses.htm

DBE Program

www.dot.il.gov/sbe/dbedir.html

Indiana

www.in.gov **(Find an Agency)**

Department of Administration

www.in.gov/idoa/2354.htm

Minority & Women's Business Enterprise (state program)

www.in.gov/idoa/2352.htm

Iowa

www.iowa.gov **(Agencies – Skip to Content – Department Listing)**

Iowa Business and Regulatory Assistance Network

http://regassist.iowa.gov/home.html

Vendor Registration

http://das.gse.iowa.gov/procurement/vendor_reg.html

Targeted Organizations (SB) Certification Program (state program) https://dia.iowa.gov/tsb

DBE Program

www.iowadot.gov/contracts/contracts_eeoaa.htm

Kansas

Department of Administration

www.da.ks.gov/purch/

Vendor Registration

www.da.ks.gov/purch/VendorRegistration.htm

DBE Program

www.ksdot.org/divadmin/civilrights/

Kentucky

Kentucky eProcurement

https://eprocurement.ky.gov/

Vendor Registration

https://emars.ky.gov/online/vss/Advantage

DBE Program

http://transportation.ky.gov/Contract/DBE/

Louisiana

Procurement & Vendor Information

www.louisiana.gov/Business/Do_Business_With_the_Stat e/

Vendor Registration

Harriet Grayson

http://wwwprd.doa.louisiana.gov/osp/lapac/vendor/Vndrmess.asp

DBE Program

http://www8.dotd.louisiana.gov/UCP/Home.aspx

Maine

Procurement & Vendor Information

www.maine.gov/portal/business/vendors.html

DBE Program

www.maine.gov/mdot/disadvantaged-business-enterprise/dbe-home.php

Maryland

eMaryland Marketplace

https://ebidmarketplace.com/default.asp

Vendor Registration

https://ebidmarketplace.com/venlogon.asp

Organizations Reserve Program (state program)

www.smallbusinessreserve.maryland.gov

DBE Program

www.mdot.maryland.gov/MBE-Program/Index.html

Massachusetts

Procurement & Access Information System

http://www.comm-pass.com/

State Office Minority & Women Business Assistance (state program)

www.somwba.state.ma.us

Michigan

Buy Michigan First

www.michigan.gov/buymichiganfirst/

Minnesota

Minnesota Materials Management Division

www.mmd.admin.state.mn.us/mn02000.htm

Vendor Registration

www.mmd.admin.state.mn.us/webven/

Targeted Group/Economically Disadvantaged (TG/ED) Organizations Program (state program)

www.mmd.admin.state.mn.us/mn02001.htm

DBE Program

www.dot.state.mn.us/civilrights/dbe.html

Mississippi

Mississippi Electronic Portal Government Contracts

www.mscpc.com

DBE Program

www.gomdot.com/Divisions/CivilRights/Resources/Progr ams/DBE/Home.aspx

Missouri

Office of Administration Division of Purchasing & Material Management

http://oa.mo.gov/purch/

Office of Supplier & Workforce Diversity (state program)

http://oa.mo.gov/oswd/

Montana

General Services Division Procurement & Vendor Information

http://gsd.mt.gov/business/default.mcpx

DBE Program

www.mdt.mt.gov/business/contracting/civil/dbe.shtml

Nebraska

Administrative Services- Materiel/Purchasing Division

www.das.state.ne.us/materiel/purchasing/

DBE Program

www.dor.state.ne.us/letting/dbeinfo.htm

Nevada

Department of Administration – Purchasing Division

http://purchasing.state.nv.us/

DBE Program

www.nevadadbe.com

New Hampshire

Department of Administrative Services – Vendor Resource Center

www.admin.state.nh.us/purchasing/vendorresources.asp

New Jersey

Department of the Treasury – Division of Purchase & Property

www.nj.gov/treasury/purchase/doingbusiness.shtml

Vendor Registration

www.state.nj.us/treasury/purchase/erfpnotifications.shtml

Minority & Women Business Enterprise (MWBE) Certification (state program)

www.nj.gov/njbusiness/contracting/minority/certification.shtml

DBE Program

www.state.nj.us/transportation/business/civilrights/dbe.shtm

New Mexico

General Services Administration – Purchasing Division

www.generalservices.state.nm.us/spd/spd.html

DBE Program

www.nmshtd.state.nm.us/main.asp?secid=11175

New York

Office of General Services - Procurement Services

www.ogs.state.ny.us/purchase/default.asp

Minority & Women Owned Business Enterprise Program (state program)

www.nylovesmwbe.ny.gov/Certification/Overview/Overview.htm

North Carolina

eProcurement Services

http://eprocurement.nc.gov/

Vendor Registration

www.ips.state.nc.us/ips/vendor/vndpubmain.asp

DBE Program

https://apps.dot.state.nc.us/vendor/directory/

North Dakota

Procurement Office

www.nd.gov/spo

Vendor Registration

www.nd.gov/spo/vendor/registry/

DBE Program

www.dot.nd.gov/divisions/civilrights/dbeprogram.htm

Ohio

State Procurement

http://procure.ohio.gov/proc/index.asp

Minority & Organizations Certification (state program)

www.development.ohio.gov/dmba/minoritysmallbusinesscert.htm

DBE Program

www.dot.state.oh.us/Divisons/EqualOpportunity/Pages/DBE.aspx

Oklahoma

Department of Central services

http://ok.gov/DCS/Central_Purchasing/index.html

Vendor Registration

www.ok.gov/DCS/Central_Purchasing/Vendor_Registration/index.html

DBE Program

www.okladot.state.ok.us/regserv/dbeinfo/index.htm

Oregon

Department of Administrative Services - Procurement Office

www.oregon.gov/DAS/SSD/SPO/index.shtml

Minority, Women & Emerging Organizations Programs (state program)

www.oregon.gov/OBDD/OMWESB/index.shtml

DBE Program

www.oregon.gov/ODOT/CS/CIVILRIGHTS/sbe/dbe/dbe_program.shtml

Pennsylvania

Department of General Services

www.dgs.state.pa.us

Rhode Island

Procurement & Vendor Information

www.ri.gov/business/index.php?subcategory=21&linkgroup=91

Organizations Enterprise Services (state program)

www.mbe.ri.gov

South Carolina

Procurement & Vendor Information

http://sc.gov/Portal/Category/DOINGBUSINESS

Small & Minority Business Enterprise Program (state program)

www.govoepp.state.sc.us/osmba/apps.html

DBE Program

www.dot.state.sc.us/doing/dbe_quarterly.shtml

South Dakota

Office of Procurement Management - Procurement & Vendor Information

www.sd.us/boa/opm/vendor_info.htm

DBE Program

www.sddot.com/operations/dbe.asp

Tennessee

Department of General Services Purchasing Division

www.tennessee.gov/generalserv/purchasing/dobusi.html

Diversity Business Enterprise Program (state program)

www.tn.gov/businessopp/index.html

DBE Program

www.tdot.state.tn.us/civil-rights/smallbusiness/

Texas

State Purchasing & Vendor Information

www.window.state.tx.us/procurement/

Historically Underutilized Business (HUB) Program

www.window.state.tx.us/procurement/prog/hub/

DBE Program

www.dot.state.tx.us/business/business_outreach/dbe.htm

Utah

Department of Administrative Services – Purchasing &Vendor Information

http://purchasing.utah.gov/vendor/index.html

Vermont

Business & Vendor Information

http://vermont.gov/portal/business/index.php?id=92

DBE Program

www.aot.state.vt.us/CivilRights/Dbe.htm

Virginia

Total e-Procurement Solution

www.eva.state.va.us/vendors/index.htm

Department of Minority Business (DMBE) Program (state program)

www.dmbe.virginia.gov

Washington State

Access – Business & Vendor information

http://acccess.wa.gov/business/dobus.aspx

Harriet Grayson

Vendor Registration

http://access.wa.gov/business/state_start.aspx

State Office of Minority & Women's Business Enterprise (state program)

www.omwbe.wa.gov

West Virginia

Purchasing Division

www.state.wv.us/admin/purchase/

DBE Program

www.state.wv.us/redirect/wvdot/wvdot.htm

Wisconsin

Bureau of Procurement

http://vendornet.state.wi.us/vendornet/default.asp

Certification Central (WISCert Central) for small, disadvantaged, minority, women and veteran (SDMWV) businesses (state program)

http://commerce.wi.gov/BD/BD-Wiscert.html

DBE Program

www.dot.wisconsin.gov/business/engrserv/dbe-main.htm

Wyoming

Administration & Information - General Services Division

http://ai.state.wy.us/GeneralServices/Procurement/index.asp

CHAPTER 4

Key Elements Enhance Government Grants Writing Success

Winning Aspects to Emphasize On an Application

Not all grant application submissions are persuasive to reviewers, nor are most funded. Obviously, some grant applications are more successful than others. It is certainly important that the grant application be written as clearly and succinctly as possible. Most granting agencies will be receiving more applications than they can possibly fund. Later in the book, there will be a detailed discussion about how to construct a winning grant proposal.

Certain elements enhance success. Of particular importance to government funders is **fiscal accountability**. Can your organization concretely demonstrate that it has in place the necessary fiscal accountability measures that will ensure that the government granting agency's dollars will be spent exactly as specified in the grant application? Private foundations usually do not audit the books of grant recipients unless the amount is huge. However, the government will audit most organizations receiving funding regardless of the amount. Even governments are audited. For example, the federal government audits state governments to ensure that the grant money was spent as specified.

How can you demonstrate fiscal accountability? In some government applications, particularly federal government applications, there will be direct questions about this issue. Don't brush off these questions with a cursory answer. Provide as much detail as possible about how these government grant funds will be segregated from other funds that the organization receives. It is of particular interest to government auditors how the organization will track personnel costs identified in the government grant application for any staff being paid out of a government grant. The organization may be required to supply detailed payroll information.

Do not apply for multiple federal government grants if the organization does not use the services of an outside accounting firm to audit the organization's books. An independent audit is of the utmost importance. The actual amount changes over time but any organizations receiving more than $500,000 from federal government grants during a one year period must have an outside auditor.

Unit Costs

Think of the government funding organization, whether federal, state or local government agency, as a smart shopper. The reviewers are looking at unit costs. Reviewers will be comparing how much product, services or outputs of some kind, can be produced among the competing applications. If your organization has the capacity to inexpensively deliver a particular program or service because it creatively uses volunteers or interns, then the organization should emphasize that fact in the grant application. Organizations where the personnel costs are high because of expansive benefits such as health insurance or retirement plans, are at a disadvantage when it comes to unit cost comparisons unless they have some other factor that minimizes these high costs. However, this alone should not discourage potential grantees from applying since the delivery of high quality, innovative or highly effective programs is important to reviewers. Cost is not the only factor. In many cases the high costs are often associated with union workers. Most government reviewers are civil servants and also union members.

Collaborations

Most federal and state government granting organizations, in their cost cutting mind-sets, need to make every dollar count so collaborations become extremely important. Some government grant applications will demand the existence and functioning of collaboration as an eligibility criterion. The eligibility criteria will spell out exactly the composition of the collaborators. For example, in a state or federal government health-related research project the collaborations could be among a local government entity, a private or public institution of higher learning and a local organization that can conduct effective community outreach. Usually these collaborations don't exist so they need to be constructed for the purposes of the grant. By submitting the grant application to the government granting organization certain demands must be met. Most commonly, the members of the collaboration must have written agreements spelling out the exact responsibilities of each member of the collaboration.

Organizations Act as Fiscal Agents for Individuals

Collaborations are often the best tool for individuals seeking to obtain government grant funding. For the organization, it is an opportunity to utilize the talents and services of an individual often by treating them as a sub-contractor or specifically acting as their fiscal agent. Most government granting agencies do not permit individuals to submit applications. For the organization, this can be a low cost alternative to having to hire specific staff for a project or program. This allows a smaller organization to leave the fiscal accountability and many personnel issues to a larger organization to manage. No organization acts as a fiscal agent without some form of financial remuneration. Usually this translates into the large organization receiving some type of indirect cost from the government agency grantor (5-20% of the total grant award).

Criteria

How does a grantor organization, public or private, determine the value of a grant submission? Some private foundations, usually the largest ones, and most government grantors develop a point system that allows them to grade each application. Most government grants are reviewed by career civil servants or recognized experts based on written criteria located within the RFP or announcement. Information required in the grant application is often assigned specific points. The actual point system will change from grant to grant, public agency vs. private foundation. However, the concept is universal. All government grantors and most large foundations need to have a reasonable objective and formal review systems in place. An actual rating sheet will be created for each applicant. Under the Freedom of Information Act the rating can be made available to the public in the case of government reviews.

A good hint for estimating the number of actual reviewers (excluding online applications) is the requirement of how many copies of the grant application to include in the submission. If you are required to send three, four, or perhaps even six copies, the number reflects the number of reviewers involved in the process.

Be sure to carefully read how the point system is allocated. For example, a recent Health & Human Services grant on Sexually Transmitted Diseases had only two categories: Plan Description (60 points) and Capacity (40 points). There were only a few questions pertaining to each of these statements in the Criteria section of the announcement. However, in the body of the RFP there were a series of far more detailed questions. It then becomes the challenge of the grant writer to incorporate all the other discussion points into these two major criteria described in the RFP.

It is quite common to have the RFP list five, six, or even more specific criteria. Typically, NIH lists five criteria: significance, approach, innovation, investigator and environment. Many NIH RFPs list the five criteria but don't specify a numerical point system. Instead, the RFP states that the reviewers will make the determination. However, the RFP will provide information on the expected "Objectives and Scope" of the proposed program/project. The areas of interest to NIH are provided in the RFP as examples of studies that are more likely to be funded.

A recent state agency RFP included a model design format. Each selection criteria was clearly listed (there were seven); and the issues to be addressed for each criteria were given. In addition, the point system was placed on the page next to each criterion listed so immediately the grant writer can determine where the reviewers are expecting the strengths of the submission to be placed. In this case, the greatest importance rested with budgetary issues.

When preparing drafts of the submission, keep reminding yourself which criteria the reviewers are emphasizing. On the draft page write the points assigned to each criterion. Imagine that you are writing a critical essay and the professor assigns points to each portion of the essay. You can get partial credit for an answer.

Family foundations and smaller private foundations do not have an elaborate point system such as the ones utilized by the big foundations or government agencies. However, the vast majority of corporate foundation grant applications do include a series of detailed questions that must be addressed as part of the application process.

Don't Agree To More Than the Organizations Can Handle

Never commit to more than your organization can complete during the grant period. This is a common mistake of inexperienced applicants. If the RFP requires that the organization provide services for up to three distinct categories of populations such as minorities, women or geographic areas with high rates of a specific disease, don't automatically conclude that your organizations must provide coverage for all three populations. There are no extra points by the reviewers if your plan is expansive, especially if the reviewers don't think the organizations can deliver on its promises. Most important of all – stay focused. You can write a better application and deliver better programs/projects if the organization seeks to serve a highly specific target population.

CHAPTER 5

Judging the Future Based on Past Performance

History & Accomplishments

Why should a private or public granting organization trust your organization with grant money? How is your organization structured and what has it accomplished in the past? These are questions that need to be addressed in any grant application.

These factors are important to weave into the basic narrative of the project. Private and public grant reviewers are not looking for Pulitzer Prize winning narratives; yet the case must be made that your organization has the experience, the necessary staff and the capacity to achieve the goals and objectives written in the grant application.

In the case of faith-based organizations, it is often essential for both private and public funders to understand the separation of the religious mission from the ability to deliver programs or projects. There are a number of foundations totally dedicated to providing funding to religious organizations. The Foundation Center (www.fdncenter.org) provides information about those specific foundations.

If it can be done, introduce the organization's official mission statement into the narrative, especially if it incorporates a compelling reason for the existence of the organization.

Uniqueness

It is common for a government agency to receive far more applications than it could possibly afford to fund. What's one way to present an appealing and winning case? How can your organization be described as unique in some fashion? Is it long-established? Is it the first in the neighborhood? Were the founders special in some measurable way? If the organization serves a special population: minorities, women, the disabled, or former prisoners; are members of these populations represented on the Board of Directors? Are staff also members of these special populations which the program/project is designed to serve? Does the organization follow a specialized training method such as day care centers that utilize Montessori techniques or the center is a member of the National Association for the Education of Young Children (NAEYC)?

It's best to find something – anything that presents a uniqueness that separates your organization from the many others. Essentially in the grant application, the grant writer is creating a marketing plan that demonstrates some degree of uniqueness.

Past Accomplishments

The best proof of the organization's ability to succeed is to analyze what the organization has done in the past. Does the organization have an enviable track record? Can the reviewers pinpoint examples of past accomplishments that will lead them to expect similar results if they award a grant to the organization? Again, the grant application will probably not ask direct questions about past accomplishments, but it will indicate places where the information needs to be introduced.

The best method of demonstrating a track history is to build a story line. When did the organization start offering this service or a complementary one? It is interesting to note if the organization started in a specific way and then proceeded to alter its course because of obstacles. This is a mark of a flexible and dynamic organization. No organization operates a program or service without problems.

If the organization offers a large number of different services, its only necessary to provide a line or two about those services. The grants writer wants to focus on past accomplishments that prove or demonstrate that the organization is capable of meeting the current grant requirements. Do not fill up the pages with superfluous information. The reviewers neither have the time nor the inclination to read pages of fluff. Focus on what the organization has done in the past that has a direct link to its ability to do something similar in the future.

If the organization has never done the specific service or program requested in the RFP, a different approach is necessary. Then the story line has to move in another direction. Why now is the organization capable of entering into a new service or program? Where specifically in its history are there similar links? Did the organization add new staff with a new set of expertise? Did the organization initiate new collaborations that allow it to enter into new territory? Did the community change and its needs shift? Is the organization moving with the community towards offering new programs and services?

The past accomplishments must be very specific. It's not enough to just indicate the organization did this or that. Give dates, places, numbers served. Does the organization have press stories that support its accomplishments? Don't send copies of the press reports; weave the information into the story line. Valuable attachments are letters of support from community leaders, and other organizations, political figures that support past accomplishments and the potential of the organization to achieve the goals and objectives in the application. It is always easier to draft a letter of support and then send it to these other organizations you want to offer letters of support. The receiving supportive organization can then modify the letter to reflect its own style. This way you can identify the strengths of the support you are seeking.

If your organization has successfully received grants, especially ones from the government or major foundations, then it's important for the new reviewers to know that information. The easiest way to display that information is by creating a simple table with the vital information such as the following: grant title, amount, which grantor agency, short phrase on purpose, and dates. Strategically, the most important visual clue in any chart or table is the upper right hand corner so make that the position of the grant with the largest amount even if it is not in chronological order.

Staff Distinctiveness

Does the organization's strength arise from its staff? One of the easiest ways of demonstrating whether the organization can meet the goals and objectives of the grant application is through the utilization of specific staff. Many grant applications will request job descriptions and resumes to accompany the application if funding is being sought for personnel. Those should be included whether or not they are requested as attachments. However, that's not enough. It is important to emphasize the skills, education, and experience of specific staff in the body of the grant submission. It should be emphasized that it's these well-honed skills that will make it possible for the organization to achieve the aims of the grant application. Not only are the past important accomplishments of the organization to be stated, but also the past achievements of specific staff. Does the staff to be associated with the proposed program or project have awards or press stories worthy of noting? Do particular staff members have interesting personal stories to weave into the grant application as supportive documentation?

The tricky issue is when there is no specific staff in place. Organizations should wait until the funding is available before they go out and hire staff. If this is the case, then it is the job description that becomes important as demonstrating proof of potential new accomplishments and the skill levels being sought in anew hire should be emphasized.

Capacity to Meet Program/Project Goals and Objectives

This is the selling point. Will the organization be able to meet its obligations? What is there about this organization, as opposed to other organizations bidding for the dollars that assures the reviewers that the money will be well spent? There may be direct questions about this issue and the grant application must address them head on with specifics.

Specifically information must be provided that addresses:

- Fiscal accountability

- Past accomplishments

- Service to the community

- Staff distinctiveness

- Measurable/reasonable goals and objectives.

- Unlike most foundation or corporate grants, the government is rarely interested whether the project is sustainable after the funding period. Government funding is usually multi-year and so it is expected that the program or service will continue for the three or five years of the funding cycle. The government doesn't assume the organizations will continue a program or service in the absence of continued government funding. However, most private funders ask how the organization will continue the funded program/project after the grant money is spent. If there is potential for revenue generation after the government funded period (e.g., fees for classes, corporate sponsorships) then that should be noted. Or perhaps a new fundraising campaign will be initiated after the grant period. If this is a possibility then it should be noted.

If sustainability is an issue for government funders, it's because the government grant funding serves as seed money. For example, if the state government provides grant funds to create or expand a day care center or a charter school, then it is expected that funding must be available after the initial period from other sources. Another example of government insistence on sustainability is when the multiyear grant requires hard cash matching funds. Typically, the grant starts with the government providing 100% of the funding and then moves to the second year where the government portion shrinks to 75% and real money is expected from the organization to the amount of 25%. By the fourth year,the government provides only 25% and the organization must come up with 75% of the funding.

CHAPTER 6

What's the Problem?

Why Should This Project/Program be Funded?

Unlike private foundation grant applications where the problems to be addressed by the grant application may be quite vague, government grants usually address specific issues and problems. In the RFP description, there may be pages of explanation why the government is interested in this problem. There is nothing to be gained by restating the obvious. However, a good government grant application will succinctly describe how it is specifically addressing what may be a recognized national or state problem. For example, the federal and state government have longed funded programs/projects addressing the learning gap between white and non-white students, health disparities between white and non-white populations and a host of social issues that distinguish the white population from non-white populations. In addition, the federal government has long offered massive amounts of grant research funds to universities and research institutes to address medical and health concerns.

"Statement of Need" Section of Grant Application

The "Statement of Need" section is the justification for why the project/program should be funded. It may or may not be directly addressed as a specific targeted section with a specified criteria numerical number; but regardless, it usually must be discussed. This section is where the grant applicant describes the community that will be served by the grant funding. The description of the problem must be very specific to the location chosen. Many corporate foundation grants ask questions about a statement of need and what specific geographic area is to be covered by the grant submission. Most corporate foundations fund grants where the corporation has operations or the bank has branch offices. So the geographic area where the grant will be having an impact is important and must be identified. Government grants often require very detailed descriptions of the community requiring real numbers from US Census or state/city planning departments about population size, ethnicity, race, gender, age, etc.

The grant application should identify physical, economic, social, financial, institutional or other problems that will be addressed by successful funding of the application. If possible create maps that pinpoint the actual geography. In a government RFP the granting agency will typically discuss the purpose of the RFP, and within this description will be the key dimensions to emphasize in a "Statement of Need" section. For example, in a recent federal RFP on childhood obesity, the statement of the problem was clearly provided. "Research has shown that obesity in childhood tracks into adulthood, carrying along with it increased susceptibility to hypertension, dyslipidemia and glucose intolerance. In fact, the striking increase in the prevalence of childhood obesity over the past 30 years has been associated with a marked increase in the incidence of type 2 diabetes among adolescents."

So the Statement of Need section submitted by a successful applicant will directly address two issues. First, demonstrate that the community has a problem by providing statistics concerning overweight children, adolescents with type 2 diabetes, adults with diabetes, etc. Also consider how the statistics have changed over the past ten or twenty years. Second, the program described in the application must be designed to meet this problem with specific interventions that are effective. Statistics should be included that identify successful interventions. If the program being considered in the grant application is entirely novel or innovative then there must be statistics to indicate positive change will occur. There must be hints or possibilities described in the literature that point in this direction. Using reputable references is important; actual citations from acceptable professional or scientific journals are encouraged.

Harriet Grayson

Use of Demographics

Every government grant application should contain some type of demographic information. The best comparisons are between the subject area and the larger community. For example, if the area under consideration is a zip code, compare this zip code with the city or county, the state and the nation if it makes the problem more pressing. Comparisons should always be included, but carefully choose which statistics make a better case. It isn't that statistics lie, but some present a more compelling story.

The most effective way of demonstrating the power of demographic analysis is graphically. It is a true adage that in using demographic information, "a picture is worth a thousand words." The easiest approach is to create graphs and tables that visually tell the story without much explanation. Microsoft's Excel software is a useful tool. It is easy to insert these tables and charts into the text if you're using Microsoft's Word software. There are many better, more sophisticated statistical packages that produce beautiful charts and tables, but may not be as easy to use. Word combined with Excel software does a nice job. The writer doesn't need to have any real knowledge of statistics or demographics to use the Excel software.

The most common graphic charts in the Excel software are column, bar, line and pie. Personal choice can determine which type of graph or chart is used, but remember that reviewers will probably be seeing the application and its attachments in black and white. Applications are usually reproduced for reviewers on black and white printers or copiers.

The Excel software column graph selections include: cluster, stacked, 100% stacked and then 3D visual effects. Again, unless the intent is to include all copies with color graphs, the 3D Versions can be distracting. The bar graphs are similar to column graphs except that the information is displayed horizontally rather than vertically. For information that looks at points over time such as monthly clinic visits over a year, daily arrests during the week, a line graph is a good pictorial choice. Using the line graph, Excel lets you then compare the geographic area under consideration with some other geography such as a city, county, state or the nation. A pie chart is also a favorite choice. It's usually easy to read and a means of displaying information in a highly descriptive manner. Practical examples of using pie charts are describing the ethnic/racial backgrounds of an area's population or results of a customer satisfaction question. The best looking pie charts use color, so remember that fact in using them in a grant application. As always when working with any type of charts, never overwhelm the reader with too many categories. It's best to keep things simple.

Where To Go

Where does the organization find reliable demographic information on items such as age, race/ethnicity, income, poverty rates and gender? Begin with local government sources. Most cities and towns maintain some demographic information on their community for use by the local Planning and Zoning Board. All state agencies also maintain detailed information on the state either in the planning department or through the economic development department. Every school district maintains detailed information about the school body: overall population of school-aged children, race, ethnicity, poverty (eligibility for free lunch), school progress, descriptions of the child's household.

The best single source of all demographic data is the US Bureau of the Census. The web site is www.census.gov. Look for the Census Bureau's "American Factfinder." After you locate that site, click on "Fact Sheet." This is a remarkable site for almost an unlimited amount of information on a large variety of demographic subjects such as population, housing, poverty, education, income, commuting to work, migration, etc. The problem is that it is not a particularly user friendly site. It takes experience to maneuver through the many sources of specific information. The 2010 Census material has been analyzed by the experts and is available (a full count of the population is conducted every ten years as required by the US Constitution). In addition to the ten year census, the US Census Bureau conducts a wide range of yearly surveys that measure economic activity, housing statistics, migration-immigration figures and overall population. The Bureau of the Census publishes yearly estimates of the population.

Other great sources of demographic information vary depending on the type of the information. For example, the federal Department of Justice is the place to go for crime statistics. There is a sub-agency that collects data of all kinds. For medical and disease information the sources are The Centers for Disease Control & Prevention (CDC) or National Institutes of Health (NIH). The federal Department of Labor surveys and publishes a wide range of labor, employment, occupational information.

Competitive Analysis – Who Else is Doing This

Although a RFP may never directly ask about anyone else in the community is doing what your organization's grant application is proposing, inevitably this is an issue. Think of the grant application as a product which will be compared to other similar products in the marketplace. If you consider the application as a marketing plan for the project/program, then assume two forms of competition: other applicants and other existing organizations or programs in the community not requesting funding. There is always a fear by all funders including the government as well as private & corporate foundations of encouraging unnecessary duplication of services.

As a part of the "Statement of Need" material, include information about other programs or organizations that are doing similar activities in the community where the program is proposed. It is rare that the activity in your proposal is unique in the community. Should this actually be the case, then make certain that the uniqueness of the program itself is prominently discussed in the grant application. If there are programs in the community that appear similar, the grant application must concretely describe how the applicant's submission is somehow different and superior to what is already available. Emphasizing the improved nature of the program is the key in effectively marketing the value of the organization's application.

Demonstration or Pilot Program

Requests for applications that specifically seek "demonstration" or "pilot programs" are truly gifts. Search out RFPs that have these twin words – demonstration project or pilot project in the titles. It usually means that the common way of dealing with this problem isn't working. The private and public funders have decided because a problem may be new (i.e., recent surge in heroin deaths by non-traditional drug abusers) or so long-entrenched that something totally innovative is needed (i.e., education gap in public schooling). It is then the organization's challenge to show that it has the talents, experiences or expertise that lends itself to successfully diving into something new. The organizations that has a reputation for successfully fostering change in the community or solving intractable problems is a viable candidate for a successful award, even if it does not have a track record with the private or public funding sources.

CHAPTER 7

The Body of the Grant Application

Tell the Story Concisely but with a Compelling Message

A grant application consists of several parts and all of them are essential in order for the grant to be even considered by reviewers. Think of the application as a book comprised of chapters. However, each chapter does not carry equal weight in a point system developed by the reviewers. Before diving into the application read and re-read the description that is the framework for the program narrative. Within the RFP, there is often a discussion of the problem or need -- the reason for the RFP. The private and public funders have decided to fund the RFP because it has accumulated information that leads the grantors to believe there is a problem that needs to be solved.

The inclusion in a government RFA of specific government sources of information reflects the government's previous investment. It is recommended that the organization, even if it is familiar with the problem, search out those references and read them. Valuable information is usually contained in the sources. If the RFP provides direct web site linkages to source material then the reviewers expect applicants to be familiar with the source material. If possible, use the source material in the program narrative. Inclusion of this material indicates that the applicant is familiar with the information. If possible, refer to or directly quote the source material as a justification for the application submission and the organization's ability to be successful at tackling the problem.

Program Narrative

The Program Narrative is the backbone of an application submission. In many cases, the grant application will require the inclusion of a section labeled "Program Narrative." There is no standard template that the organization can use for this section. However, the rationale for the application submission is contained in this section.

Instructions

There are always instructions that accompany the "Program Narrative" section. Follow the instructions precisely. The instructions often require seemingly insignificant requisites but pay attention to all of them. Typically these instructions include: maximum length of the document, paging, font size, spacing and margins of each page, organization's name on each page or the opposite -- no name on the pages. If the document is not sent electronically then there will be requirements about the number of copies as well as original signatures.

The page length requirement for the "Program Narrative" is a very important starting point. There are rarely a minimum number of pages required but often the maximum is clearly stated. The page length of the Narrative varies dramatically. (Applications can be as short as 2-3 pages or as long as 50 pages.) In general, private and corporate foundation grant application submissions are less lengthy than government applications. Usually the amount of money being requested is considerably different. Typically, a federal government grant applicant is seeking funding of at least $25,000 while private or corporate grant requests can be as small as $500. Large major foundations have an application and page requirements similar to the government in both size and scope.

Program Narrative requirements vary in complexity. Large major foundations and the government are more similar while family, private and corporate foundation Program Narratives are generally simple and straight forward. As a rule, the "Program Narrative" section is open to the interpretation of the submitting applicant. There may be some questions to be addressed but few can be answered with just "Yes" or "No." The narrative is a like a school paper – it is left to the imagination of the writer to describe the problem, specifically indicate how to solve it, and follow-up with a plan on how to evaluate the success of the venture.

Executive Summary

Sometimes the "Program Narrative" requires the inclusion of an Executive Summary, Program Summary or an Abstract. Write the summary last because it will then be easier to summarize the proposed program/project. The request for an Abstract may also include restrictions; usually it is framed as a summary description of 250 words or less. Use the 'Word Count' tool in Microsoft's Word software to ensure that the Abstract is the proper length.

The Executive Summary usually has restrictions. Typically, the summary should be one page in length or no more than two pages. As always with any given restrictions, follow them precisely.

Key Sections

One can expect that the "Program Narrative" should contain information on the need for the program/project. However, there may be a distinct and separate section called 'Statement of Need'. Then there is the marketing of the organization; why your Organization is the perfect instrument for solving the problem. This is usually followed by a detailed discussion of the goals and objectives and the specific actions the organization will undertake to implement the goals and objectives.

Usually a "Program Narrative" will also require some kind of 'Evaluation Plan'. The government and major foundations will require a detailed evaluation plan. Sometimes the federal government has hired an outside firm to conduct the evaluation. The applicant just needs to budget for the costs associated with contributing to the evaluation (i.e., personnel, data collection, and time allocation). Private and corporate foundations will require an evaluation but it can usually be conducted internally and at a minimum cost.

If the organization does not have the expertise to write a grant application, and is so cash strapped that it is unable to pay for the services of an outside grant writer, you may be able to actually fund the grants writer by providing funding through the evaluation plan. In some instances an effective grants writer can also serve as the evaluator.

A "Program Narrative" may require a 'Management Plan'. Here it is important to highlight the specific talents, experiences and expertise of all the individuals involved in the program/project. The 'Management Plan' may require providing organizational charts with designated lines of authority.

Also, Program Narratives can have quirky requirements. One may require a 'Table of Contents' especially if the narrative is lengthy. Others require the completion and inclusion of special tables and charts. Some narratives permit the grant writer to reconstruct a table or chart to make it easier to complete if there isn't any way to electronically access the table. State government grant applications are particularly lengthy if the funding agency expects many small and mid-size organizations to apply for funding. Experience has demonstrated that smaller organizations can have difficulty completing all the actions they promised in their grant application. So to ensure that the work is done on time and within budget, the state funding agency will require the completion of many forms and ask many questions.

Prepare an Outline or Check List

This is a suggestion, particularly for an organization that has never previously applied for outside grant funding. Start by reading and diagramming the essential points described in the RFP. Create a check list that includes questions you may have as you read the grant application.

Most funders, private and public, will answer your questions about the grant application and the process. The contact names for private or corporate foundations are usually located on the foundation's web site. There may also be a phone number provided or an email address.

Most government grant applications include the name(s) of contact people (phone number, email address). These people are your new best friends. You cannot pester these people with repeated questioning. But as part of the check list you should compile a list of questions and submit it to the contact people at one time. The federal government often has a proscribed "Comment Period" during which you can submit your questions regarding the grant application or the process. Beyond that comment period the government will not accept questions. If the government grant application required or permitted a Letter of Intent LOI), all questions received and answered will be automatically forwarded to all organizations that submitted the LOI. The outline can assist the grant writer in determining what specific information is required, where in the application to insert the information or demographic tables as well as what attachments should be included in constructing a successful application.

The outline is a guide in constructing the winning and compelling story about the program/project. It need not be elaborate but it should assist the grant writer in the construction of the Program Narrative.

Actually, some grant submissions require the completion and inclusion of a prepared "Checklist" while others simply include a checklist as a guide to the grant writer.

Goals and Objectives

This section is often hastily constructed resulting in the program/project being rejected. Consider this section as the tool which reviewers go through and determine whether the program/project is feasible. The goals and/or objectives, (different funders can use different terminology but with the same intent), are essentially the plan on how the organization intends to meet the problem addressed earlier in the Program Narrative.

If the information in the RFP speaks to the funder's specific goals and objectives, such as increasing financial literacy or reducing violent youth gang crime, then the grant submission should include addressing the funders' goals. Most government funders provide referenced information in the Announcement section of the RFP, the sources cited are usually government reports that mention the federal or state's overall goals and objectives. If you can incorporate these government goals and objectives into the program/project being proposed, it demonstrates the organization's familiarity with the problem.

The RFP expects that the goals and objectives are measurable and can be completed in specific time frames. Sometimes the RFP will suggest or require that this information be detailed in a table format. If possible, even if not requested, construct the goals and objectives in an easy to read table. This will force the grant writer to quickly ascertain the logic of the goals and objectives as well as the actions to be taken. Staring at all the vital information in a table format makes it easier to notice timing issues or the sequencing of events.

A model table can be constructed that lists each goal or objective followed by specific actions that will be taken, when these actions will occur, which individuals will be responsible or involved in the actions, how it will be measured and how it will be evaluated. The timetable can be either be in months or quarters depending on the nature of the grant submission.

Speak to the Language of the RFP

Use the jargon that is cited in the RFP. Private and corporate foundations are less likely to use any jargon. But each government agency has its own specific language and these words need to be repeated in the grant submission. The government is famous for its use of acronyms and assumes that anyone responding to a RFP will be familiar with its use of language. Acronyms and jargon are just shorthand and if you want to join the club then it is expected you are well versed in the language.

Again, if government sources are cited in the RFP, read them and use them in the grant submission. Use information from government sites in developing the goals and objectives section as your organization's plan to further the government's goal to reduce a problem or change a situation or create a new environment. In creating the Program Narrative also consider the reviewers stated "Criteria" in the RFP.

The trick in developing an effective grant application in response to a RFP is thinking like the reviewers. How would you rate the application? Essentially, the grant writer is weaving a good story, using the language of the RFP, reinforcing the funder's interests in certain areas and gaining the most points by effectively building on the criteria enumerated in the RFP. It is often helpful to have an outside person read the grant submission to ensure it is building an effective story and the flow is logical.

CHAPTER 8

Writing the Budget   Does the Organizations have a feasible financial plan?

Nothing is more essential than a carefully constructed budget based on realistic numbers and a justification for all the dollars requested. Private and corporate foundations do not require highly sophisticated budgets but justification and real numbers for the items to be funded. State government grant budgets usually follow the budget categories of federal government grants.

The federal application process usually requires that specific forms be completed and submitted with the grant submission. Form 424A – 'Budget Information – Non-Construction Programs' is a two page form that is not difficult to complete. However, the tough part is carefully crafting a budget that passes the federal reviewers' feasibility analysis. Has the organization created a budget that reflects the costs of developing a program/project and will the award amount permit the successful implementation of the goals and objectives described in the Program Narrative? Instructions for the SF (Standard Form) 424A are provided on-line.

The budget categories or 'object class categories' are listed on the Form 424A. They are ordinary categories one would use in any budget: personnel, fringe benefits, travel, equipment, supplies, contractual, construction, other. This particular form 424A includes a category labeled construction but it is to be used when the applicant is not requesting federal government funding for construction purposes. If construction is required but will be paid by other than non-federal government funding it is to be listed on Form 424A. In the case where the applicant is seeking federal government funding for construction purposes, use Form 424C 'Budget Information – Construction Programs.'

In developing a budget, the two major categories are personnel costs that may represent the majority of the expenses and

OTPS – Other than Personnel Services. What is important to all funders, whether private, corporate or government reviewers, is whether the program can be adequately funded. Does the applicant intend to use other sources of funding beyond the grant including program income – revenue?

Private and corporate funders often assume that the grant funding is only seed money and that the program will last because the organization will be able to sustain the program into the future with other fiscal sources. Often these questions are directly asked of the applicant. How will this program be sustained? As a result of viewing the grant as only a one year funded project,the budget information submitted is often only a simple Excel software spreadsheet.

The government does not think in the same way. Programs grant funded by either state or federal government sources most often assume that without government funding the program will cease to exist. The grant is often for multiple years and so at a minimum, two year detailed budgets are required. There is also often a requirement to estimate budgets for the entire grant funded period (2-7 years depending upon the exact grant).

The online federal grant application requires completion of quarterly budgets for two years. State government grants often follow this same pattern since most of the original money was from the federal government. The easiest method is to simply divide the requested funding by four. However, that approach may not be the most appropriate based on how costs are expected to be spent. Whether or not the budget is assigned a high number of points (20% or more of total points is considered significant) under the selection criteria, government reviewers will carefully scrutinize the budget. Do not be misled by the simple forms, the budget is one of the most decisive pieces of the grant submission.

As of 2005, if the organization is receiving $500,000 or more annually in grant funding from the federal government, the organization must prepare and submit the infamous A-133 Audit. This is an expensive audit that must be prepared by a highly competent, outside auditing firm familiar with the rules and regulations concerning the A-133 Audit. It is reasonable to expect that the cost of such an audit can range from $20,000-$25,000. The dollar amount triggering an A-133 Audit has been steadily rising. The dollar amount is based on totaling all federal government awards for the year so that two awards of $250,000 apiece will trigger the A-133 Audit.

Personnel Services

This is often a key component of the budget for larger grants ($25,000 or more). For small grants (less than $5,000), particularly private and corporate foundation grants, there is usually no personnel component. The grant may provide for some sub-contracting of individuals especially for training or artistic services. The inclusion of personnel costs as part of the grant budget assumes that without adequate funding for the personnel listed in the grant submission, the program/project cannot move forward.

Should the organization receive funding, in constructing the project/program budget, start with the direct personnel responsible. If there is an incumbent in the position, typically a grant application will require a resume. If the position is new or vacant, the grant submission should include a job description for each position. In developing the budget, think in terms of position title, percentage of time each position will be dedicated to the program/project based on a 12 month period, and the salary/fringe benefits for each position. Then consider how the position will be funded – what sources will the organization be tapping to cover the costs of each position. For example, the position of Program Coordinator (title), will be dedicated to the project 100% of the time for 12 months. Now will the Program Coordinator position be funded 100% from this grant application? Or will the position require funding from other sources such as program revenue, other federal or state funds, or fundraising sources?

WARNING: If the organization intends to fund a position from more than one government source, be warned that the decision will raise a red flag for government fiscal reviewers. Government auditors are concerned with the issue of supplanting of government funds. What that means is the government thinks an organization is double dipping, paying for the same position twice from two separate government sources.

It is obvious that if an organization uses government funds, all expenditures must be carefully recorded; recordkeeping must be of the highest quality. Sometimes an organization provides documentation for each piece of equipment purchased and all printing and mailing, but then fails to maintain adequate personnel records. Be certain that personnel pay documentation is kept and clearly indicates the position's time spent on any government funded program/project.

Fiscal reviewers for private and corporate foundations are less strict about accounting practices. However, all funds from grant sources even if the amount is small (less than $5,000) should be segregated from the organization's operating accounts.

Indirect Costs

Every government grant application is different regarding the acceptability of including indirect costs in the budget. The finance people in the organization will appreciate the value of using indirect costs, but in preparing the budget, read all the fine print concerning this issue. Being able to include this in a grant is considered a gift by most finance people, since it can cover general administrative costs seldom directly funded. This includes the accounting or legal staff, rental space, utilities and telephone. Private and corporate foundation grants rarely offer in-direct cost allowances.

If the organization is receiving or actively seeking government funding for a variety of programs/projects, the finance staff should consider negotiating with the government an acceptable, indirect rate. The advantage of such an agreed upon rate is that if the grant submission permits it, the organization simply plugs in the rate. However, if the rate is low then it may not be advisable to always use the same rate for each program/project. This is something the grant writer and the financial staff should discuss.

Also, the indirect cost is usually based on a specific percentage, but with strings attached. For example, the grant may state within the budgetary description in the RFP that an applicant can use an indirect expense of 10 percent. The 10 percent refers to expenses that have been approved by the government grant fiscal staff. So the organization may assume that a grant of $100,000 with an indirect cost of 10% automatically means there is $10,000 to offset the costs of the accounting and legal staff of the organization. This is not necessarily true in all cases. If the organization purchases a piece of equipment for $5,000 but the government agency fiscal staff rejects that expense (and this can happen), the indirect cost will be based on 10 percent of $95,000 ($9,500) unless you can find a $5,000 cost that is acceptable to the government fiscal staff.

WARNING – Even if the grant award budget lists equipment or supplies, do not spend the money until the organization receives specific, written approval for those items. The most common problem occurs over personnel expenses. An individual may leave the organization and there is a vacancy, and subsequently savings in the grant award. Get permission to redirect the personnel money to another purpose before moving forward and spending the money. That can also mean getting permission to pay the salary and fringe benefits of a new hire or a transfer within the organization.

In-Kind-Costs/Matching Requirements

The mandated inclusion of a matching funds requirement can be a deciding factor in whether to go forward and submit a grant application. A smaller organization should read the RFP carefully regarding this issue before moving ahead. Talk with the finance staff. If there is a matching requirement, the fiscal staff needs to carefully examine what types of costs will satisfy the matching requirements. Government grants sometimes have matching requirements especially if it's a construction grant. Private and corporate foundations don't usually have matching requirements if the grant period is only for one year or small (less than $5,000). A matching requirement may be necessary if the grant period is two years or more.

In some cases, a federal government award cannot be matched by another federal government grant or any federal funds, while in other cases there are no restrictions. The tricky part about using other government funds for matching purposes is knowing exactly the source of that funding. For example, state government grant awards are often based on awards from the federal government. If there is restriction on the use of federal funding for matching purposes then check carefully the source of any state or local money. Although the award letter comes from the state or local government award, it may still be unacceptable. The best source of advice for these technical matters is the contacts that are listed in the RFP.

An organization can expect that if the RFP speaks about challenge grants, then matching will be required. Challenge grants are issued by private, corporate and government funding sources. The issue is usually that the amount of money the organization has to match grows while the foundation or government contribution declines. The purpose in these changing financial requirements is to make the program/project self-sufficient because by design there are potential revenue streams or other fundraising possible. Ordinarily the match must also be actual money and not in-kind.

Restrictions

Private and corporate foundations include restrictions on the types of activities that are permissible to be funded with the grant money. Typically, these restrictions have to do with fundraising activities and sometimes operating expenses.

There are rarely government grants without restrictions. There are two types of restrictions that require careful review by an organization. First, restrictions on activities the RFP will fund. These types of restrictions can be activities such as training when the RFP speaks about implementation. If the grant is successfully awarded, it may be that costs associated with training will be rejected. Second, there are usually restrictions on fundable expenditures. Every grant

will be different but almost all have some type of budget restriction Carefully read what the grant will **NOT** pay for in the RFP. Th usual "no-no's" are expenses linked to items such as travel and for (federal grants usually restrict the per person costs for meals). F example, the federal government will not pay for first class airpla travel. The government has an acceptable vehicle reimbursement ra and accepts no other rate. The restrictions can be much m formidable. If there is a question, discuss the issue with 1 government contact person. There are usually two different types contacts listed in the RFP; a program contact and a fiscal cont; These people should become your new best friends.

Individuals are commonly excluded from directly receiv grant funding whether it's private, corporate or government fund However, that restriction can be ameliorated by honest ingent The organization can function as a fiscal agent for an individual other cases using the fiscal agent concept, the individual is hired consultant for the program/project.

CHAPTER 9

Rejection - The rejection letter is only the beginning

The government as well as private and corporate funders actually appreciate an organization that is willing to try more than once. No is never the end of the discussion. Private sources (private or corporate foundations) are under no obligation to provide information about why the grant was rejected. Most will permit anyone to view those projects/programs that were funded. Usually a corporation will release a press release with the information.

However, the government is under an obligation to provide information about the program/project's rejection. How much information is provided will vary from agency to agency. In some cases, the government reviewers will include a letter detailing the shortcomings of a grant application. If a letter does not provide any specific reasons for the denial, there is nothing lost by making a call or sending an e-mail to one of the RFP contacts listed. The organization's first effort may not have secured enough points. An organization can ask how many points it earned from the reviewers.

Consider the denial letter as a first step in seeking funding from other grant sources. The organization has now gained the experience of applying and should have learned some things about the process or enough of it. The organization has an easier time completing all the application forms. In the case of the federal government, the cumbersome on-line process has been completed. A denial letter can provide the basis for the next application.

While we would like to think that if we wrote a more compelling story the grant would have been funded, rarely is it that simple. Most of the time, the rejection has to do with the implementation plan (carrying out the goals and objectives) or the budget. The reviewers did not have faith that the information

provided in the grant application was sufficient to assure that the plan would be carried out in a timely fashion. In some cases, the plan was simply not what the reviewers were looking for in an application. The plan was outside the parameters described in the grant guidelines. Other typical shortcomings have to do with budgetary concerns or the expertise/experience of staff.

For the next try, re-examine the budget and look for ways to trim unit costs. The organization's staff may earn more experience through a training course or new degree. Look for RFPs or grant guidelines that seem to require similar expertise or areas of interest as the submitted grant application.

Another common problem is the failure to secure the appropriate outside support, if a partnership or coalition was required. This is the time to continue working on creating a more viable group, which can collaboratively apply for more grants.

In most instances, government grantors will list those that were successfully funded. There may be a useful description of the actual winning grant applications or even a copy of the actual successfully applications. Carefully examine the available materials. Look for similar programs/projects but also the geographic distribution of the winning grant applications. Private, corporate and government grantors have a certain obligation to spread around the wealth. If there are no winning applications from your community, it can work in your organization's favor at a future attempt. The federal government reviewers probably don't want to neglect a particular area too many times. At the same time, if the community has a very successful model in place there may be no point in re-applying.

It isn't until an organization actually competes for private, corporate and government funding that it can truly appreciate the winners. As always with funding, never discount the power of politics. It is often who you know not what you know that actually matters. For that reason, it is highly recommended to ensure that all elected politicians representing the organization's geographic area be fully aware of the work and mission of your organization.

Harriet Grayson

CHAPTER 10

In Conclusion

Awards Keep Coming Regardless of Economic Times

Good luck with writing your grant proposal. There are opportunities out there for organization of all kinds. Do not get discouraged if your proposal is rejected; remember the advice from the first line of this book. The United States government has billions of dollars earmarked for grants. With determination and a well-organized proposal, your grant proposal can succeed.

Private, corporate and government priorities shift so that grant opportunities never disappear but changes are likely. A new CEO, the retirement of a long-time foundation head or a new federal administration or a new Congress can set new priorities. There will never be enough funding to meet every request by the thousands of organizations in the country seeking financial assistance.

The best approach is to design a funding strategy that looks at the many varied potential sources of funding that an organizations can successfully obtain. A well-constructed and comprehensive strategy requires understanding that funding must be diverse especially if it's directed at a specific proposal or program. The following sources are only suggestions for your search:

- Federal Government

- State Government

- City/County/Local Government

- Corporate Foundations

- Private Foundations

- Family Foundations

- Individual Donations/Sponsors

- Revenues – Bidding for Government Contracts

Searching for funding support is more an art than a science and it is a wise approach to look everywhere. While the internet is becoming the tool to use for researching where to find grants, unfortunately it is does not capture all government grant application information, especially on the state and local level.

The organization needs to find someone (best case scenario a volunteer or intern) to review all the announcements and information that is available. A knowledgeable person must read through the materials to determine whether the grant announcement is something worth pursuing. Use this book as a resource while researching and writing a proposal. We live in a fast paced world so be prepared and nimble as you cast out a net for potential sources of private, corporate and government grant funding.

Appendix A: Grant & Contracting Glossary

Explanation of Grant & Contracting Terminology

Acquisition is the acquiring of supplies or services by a government agency with appropriated funds through purchase or lease.

Applicant is the entity requesting a grant.

Applicant notice is published on Grants.gov and invited applications for one or more discretionary grant competitions. It provides basic program and fiscal information on each competition, informs potential applicants when and where they can obtain applications, and cites the deadline date for a particular competition.

Application Package is a group of specific forms and documents for a specific funding opportunity which are used to apply for a grant.

Assurances are a variety of requirements, found in different Federal laws, regulations and executive orders, which applicants agree in writing to observe as a condition of receiving federal assistance.

Authorized Organization Representative (AOR) is the individual who submits a grant on behalf of a company, organization, institution or government. Only an AOR has the authority to sign and submit grant applications.

Award is financial assistance that provides support or stimulation to accomplish a public purpose. Awards include grants and other agreements in the form or money or property in lieu of money, by a grantor agency to an eligible recipient. The term does not include: technical assistance, which provides services instead of money; other assistance in the form of loans, loan guarantees, interest subsidies, or insurance; direct payments of any kind to individuals; and contracts.

Benefits.gov is a federal website created in 2002 to provide citizens with easy online access to government benefit and assistance programs. Information provided includes on citizen tax filing, federal rulemaking, electronic training, and benefit information delivery.

Budget period is an interval of time into which a project period is divided for budgetary purposes.

Budget narrative explains the budget. Explanations can include the derivation of amounts, the itemization of totals, the purpose of purchased supplies and services, and the justification of the size of salaries, fringe benefits, and indirect costs.

Catalog of Federal Domestic Assistance (CFDA) lists all domestic assistance programs of the Federal Government. It includes information about a program's authorization, fiscal details, accomplishments, regulations, guidelines, eligibility requirements, information contacts, and application and award process. It is maintained by the General Services Administration. It can be found on the web at www.cfda.gov.

Certificate of Competency is a certificate issued by the Organizations Administration (SBA) stating that the holder is "responsible" in terms of capability, competency, capacity, credit, integrity, perseverance, and tenacity for the purpose of receiving and performing a specific government contract.

Certified 8(a) Firm is a firm owned and operated by socially and economically disadvantaged individuals and eligible to receive federal contracts under the SBA 8(e) Business Development Program.

Contractor Team Arrangement is an arrangement in which (a) two or more companies form a partnership or joint venture to act as potential prime contractor; or (b) an agreement by a potential prime contractor with one or more other companies to have them act as its subcontractors under a specified government contract or acquisition program.

Cost sharing or matching is the portion of project or program costs not borne by the grantor agency.

Deadline date is the date by which a discretionary grant application must be received by a grantor agency in order for it to be considered for funding.

Discretionary grant is an award of financial assistance in the form of money by a grantor agency to an eligible grantee, usually made on the basis of a competitive review process.

DUNS Number is a nine-digit number assigned to an organization by Dun & Bradstreet (D & B) and required to successfully transmit electronic on-line federal grant applications.

E-Business Point of Contact (E-Biz POC) is responsible for the administration and management of grant activities in his/her organization. The E-Biz POC authorizes representative of their organization (AOR) to submit grant applications through Grants.gov. An E-Biz POC must also register as an AOR to submit an application.

Emerging Organizations is a Organizations concern whose size is no greater than 50 percent of the numerical size standard applicable to the Standard Industrial Classification (SIC) code assigned to a contracting opportunity.

FedBizOpps.gov is the single point-of-entry for commercial vendors and government buyers to post, search, monitor and retrieve opportunities solicited by the entire federal contracting community.

Federal Acquisition Regulation (FAR) is the body of regulations which is the primary source of authority governing the government procurement process, The FAR, which is published as Chapter 1 of Title 48 of the Code of Federal Regulations, is prepared, issued and maintained under the joint auspices of the

Secretary of Defense, the Administrator of General Services Administration, and the Administrator of the National Aeronautics and Space Administration.

Federal register is a daily compilation of Federal regulations and other Federal agency documents of public interest including competitive grant proposals prepared by the National Archives and Records Administration.

Funding Opportunity Announcement is a publicly available document by which a federal agency makes known its intentions to award discretionary grants or cooperative agreements, usually as a result of competition for funds. Funding opportunity announcements may be known as program announcements, notices of funding availability, request for proposals, solicitations or other names depending on the agency and type of program. Funding opportunity announcements can be found at Grants.gov/FIND and on the internet at the funding agency's or program's website.

Funding Opportunity Number is the number that a federal agency assigns to its grant announcement.

Grant is an award of financial assistance, the principal purpose of which is to transfer a thing of value from a grantor agency. A grant is distinguished from a contact, which is used to acquire property or services for the grantor's direct benefit or use.

Grantee is an individual or organization that has been awarded financial assistance by a grantor agency.

Grants.gov is a storefront web portal for use in electronic collection of data (forms and reports) for federal grant-making agencies through the Grants.gov site (www.grants.gov).

Indirect cost rate is a percentage established by an agency for a grantee organization, which the grantee uses in computing the dollar amount it charges to the grant to reimburse itself for indirect costs incurred in doing the work of the grant project.

Local Government is a local unit of government, including specifically a county, municipality, city, town, township, local public authority, school district, special district, intro-sate district, council of governments, or any other regional or interstate entity.

Marketing Partner ID (MPIN) is a personal code that allows you to access federal government applications and acts as your password. You make up the code and register it in SAM. The MPIN must have 9 digits containing at least one alpha character (must be in capital letters) and one number (no spaces or special characters permitted).

North American Industry Classification System (NAICS) Code is a code with a maximum of six digits used to classify business establishments. This code will be replacing the Standard Industrial Classification (SIC) code.

Organization is a grant applicant who is submitting a grant on behalf of a company, state, local or tribal government, academic or research institution, not-for-profit, or any other type of institution.

PDF is a file format designed to enable printing and viewing of documents with all their formatting (typefaces, images, layout, etc.) appearing the same regardless of what operating system us used, so a PDF document should look the same on Windows, Macintosh, Linux, OS/2.

Point of Contact (POC) is an individual who is designated as the person responsible for authorization and maintenance of information on behalf of a registrant, coordinating communication among organizations.

Profile is applicant information stored in the Grants.gov system for the purpose of identifying a user.

Project Period is the period established in the award document during which awarding agency sponsorship begins and ends.

Request for Application (RFA) is a type of solicitation notice in which an organization announces that grant funding is available, and allows researchers and other organizations to present bids on how the funding could be used.

Request for Proposal (RFP) is a solicitation made, often through a bidding process, by an agency or company interested in procurement of a commodity, service or valuable asset, to potential suppliers to submit business proposals.

Organizations Innovative Research (SBIR) is a grant/contract designed to foster technological innovation by organizations with 500 or fewer employees. The SBIR contract program provides for a three-phased approach to research and development projects: technological feasibility and concept development; the primary research effort; and the conversion of the technology to a commercial application.

Standard Form 424 (SF-424) Series Forms include the following:

SF-424 (Application for Federal Assistance cover page)

SF-424A (Budget Information Non-construction Programs)

SF-424B (Assurances Non-construction Programs)

SF-424C (Budget Information Construction Programs)

SF-424D (Assurances Construction Programs)

Third Party In-kind Contributions is the value of non-cash contributions provided by third parties. Third party in-kind contributions may be in the form of real property, equipment, supplies and other expendable property, and the value of goods and services directly benefiting and specifically identifiable to the project or program.

MEET HARRIET GRAYSON

Harriet Grayson is an accomplished writer, speaker and presenter. She has worked in the public, private and non-profit worlds over a professional career that has included years as an urban planner, insurance executive, non-profit grants writer and entrepreneur.

Educated at Queens College (Flushing, NY, BA), NYU's Wagner School of Public Administration (Masters of Urban Planning) and the University of Denver (MA). She has been an adjunct professor teaching at a variety of colleges in CO, CT and MA courses on planning and sociology/demography, marketing, grants writing and fundraising topics.

She is the President of 5 Star Seminars (www.5starseminars.com) based in southern New England. Through her company she teaches seminars on grants writing and fundraising topics. In addition, 5 Star Seminars provides consulting services on researching & writing grants for a variety of governmental entities as well as non-profit organizations.

Ms. Grayson is also an independent publisher of Ocean Breeze Press based in Westerly, RI (www.oceanbreezepress.com). The company offers a variety of titles in Non-Fiction, Fiction and Poetry divisions.

She is also a host/producer of a public access TV show called Community Culture Showcase (www.communitycultureshowcase.weebly.com). The TV show appears weekly in southeast Ct and RI with the aim of encouraging and promoting the arts and culture of the local communities. She recently completed the documentary "Aftermath" which chronicled the destruction and rebuilding of iconic Misquamicut Beach in RI devastated by Super Storm Sandy.

OCEAN BREEZE PRESS – The voice of independent publishing

Ocean Breeze Press
(www.oceanbreezepress.com)

Offers a variety of titles for all tastes:

Non-Fiction

"Guide to Grants Writing for Non-Profits" by **Harriet Grayson**

"Government Opportunities for Small Business" by **Harriet Grayson**

Coming in Fall 2014

"Guide to Special Events Planning for Non-Profits" by **Harriet Grayson**

Fiction

"Loose Ends" by Anastasia Goodman

First in a series of Sasha Perlov mysteries about Russian American NYPD detective as he solves crimes among his fellow immigrants. A dead man is found in a Brighton Beach house, his widow is there but she doesn't understand English so Sasha Perlov and his partner Jimmy Sutton are called to the scene. Who if anyone is responsible for the man's death? Sasha is a man who straddles both worlds – traveling between the Russian Motherland and his new home in the New Jerusalem, New York.

Coming Soon in 2014

"Terror in Brooklyn" by **Anastasia Goodman**

The second in the Sasha Perlov mysteries. A Hasidic man from the former Central Asian republic of Uzbekistan of the former Soviet Union is murdered in the streets of Brooklyn. Sasha and his partner Jimmy Sutton are called to the case. It's not a case of a street mugging but evolves into a case of international intrigue.

Poetry

"For If Dreams Die" by Stacey Leigh collection of poetry by new poet

ORDER NOW

www.oceanbreezepress.com or via www.amazon.com

www.ingramcontent.com/pod-product-compliance
Lightning Source LLC
Chambersburg PA
CBHW070213290526
45789CB00002B/983